Nine Fruits of the Spirit

of the Spirit

A Bible Study on Developing Christian Character

Love

Robert Strand

New Leaf Press

A Division of New Leaf Publishing Group

First printing: June 1999
Third printing: September 2009

ISBN-13: 978-0-89221-461-7
ISBN-10: 0-89221-461-9
Library of Congress Number: 99-64007

Cover by Janell Robertson

Printed in China

Please visit our website for other great titles:
www.newleafpress.net

For information regarding author interviews, please contact the
publicity department at (870) 438-5288.

Contents

Introduction 5

The Fruit of the Spirit Is . . . Love 9

Let's Define Love 11

Loving Others 17

Some of the Marks of Love as a
    Fruit of the Spirit 25

The Practical Application of the
    Truth We Have Discovered 31

A Love That Forgives 37

A Life Application of This Principle
    of Forgiving Love in Action 46

A Love That Lasts Forever! 47

In Summary 55

Introduction

There is an ancient story out of the Middle East which tells of three merchants crossing the desert. They were traveling at night in the darkness to avoid the heat of the day. As they were crossing over a dry creek bed, a loud attention-demanding voice out of the darkness commanded them to stop. They were then ordered to get down off their camels, stoop down and pick up pebbles from the creek bed, and put them into their pockets.

Immediately after doing as they had been commanded, they were then told to leave that place and continue until dawn before they stopped to set up camp. This mysterious voice told them that in the morning they would be both sad and happy. Understandably shaken, they obeyed the voice and traveled on through the rest of the night without stopping. When morning dawned, these three merchants anxiously looked into their pockets. Instead of finding the pebbles as expected, there were precious jewels! And, they were both happy and sad. Happy that they had picked up some of the pebbles, but sad because they hadn't gathered more when they had the opportunity.

This fable expresses how many of us feel about the treasures of God's Word. There is coming a day when we will be thrilled because we have absorbed as much as we have, but sad because we had not gleaned much more. Jewels are best shown off when held up to a bright light and slowly turned so that each polished facet can catch and reflect the light.

Each of these nine jewels of character will be examined in the light of God's Word and how best to allow them to be developed in the individual life. That is how I feel about the following three verses from Paul's writings which challenge us with what their Christian character or personality should look like. Jesus Christ has boiled down a Christian's responsibility to two succinct commands: Love the Lord your God with all your heart, mind, soul, and body, and love your neighbor like yourself. Likewise, Paul the apostle has captured for us the Christian personality in nine traits:

> But the fruit of the Spirit is love, joy, peace, patience, kindness, goodness, faithfulness, gentleness, and self-control. Against such things there is no law. Those who belong to Christ Jesus have crucified the sinful nature with its passions and desires. Since we live by the Spirit, let us keep in step with the Spirit (Gal. 5:22–25).

At the very beginning of this study, I must point out a subtle, yet obvious, distinction. The "fruit" of the Spirit is a composite description of what the Christian lifestyle and character traits are all about — an unbroken whole. We can't pick only the fruit we like.

Unlocked in these nine portraits are the riches of a Christ-centered personality. The thrill of the search is ahead of us!

Love

AGAPE, (Greek), meaning: God's fruit
of love which gives itself away with a
pure motive and most generously.

THE FRUIT OF THE
SPIRIT IS . . . LOVE

Miracles can be counterfeited and gifts can be imitated. History is full of examples of such pseudo-religious pretenders. But the fruit of the Spirit cannot be imitated! Why? Because the fruit of the Spirit is manifested by what a person is and not what a person does! Jesus Christ forever set the record straight when He said, "By their fruits you shall know them!" This fruit is internal and eternal-lasting, while miracles will fade.

The most important part of the message which Jesus preached and which His followers taught is that God is concerned about what is on the inside and the further development of these traits through the Spirit. The power of Christ was not really in the miracles which He performed but rather in the message which He left for us.

Our day is marked by the pseudo, the unreal, the false, the spin, and virtual reality which is not real at all. We shall be known and remembered by what we are rather than what we do. How about following this for a lifestyle principle?

"Your beauty should not come from outward adornment.... Instead, it should be that of your inner self, the unfading beauty of a gentle and quiet spirit, which is of great worth in God's sight" (1 Pet. 3:3–4).

LET'S DEFINE LOVE

There are hundreds of definitions of love — but what does the Bible have to say about love and how is it to be defined and lived out?

Let's start with reading 1 Corinthians 13:4–13.

In your own life — how has love's true meaning been confused?

_____

_____

_____

_____

_____

_____

_____

_____

Name the major positive characteristics which show what love is and does.

_____

_____

_____

_____

Name what love is not and does not do.

_____

_____

_____

_____

How long-lasting is this kind of love?

_____

_____

_____

_____

Think of someone you know who is loving. Name some of the specific ways in which he or she demonstrates love to and for others.

_____

_____

_____

_____

_____

What are the gifts of the Spirit which Paul calls attention to in this entire chapter?

_____

_____

_____

_____

_____

Why are the gifts worth nothing without love?

_____

_____

_____

_____

Compare the development of the fruit in the life of a believer with
that of the maturing of a child.

_____

_____

_____

_____

Why do you think that love is listed as the greatest?

_____

_____

_____

_____

Now that you have looked at and listed the qualities of love, which one are you in the most need of working on in your life?

_____

_____

_____

_____

Why?

_____

_____

_____

_____

_____

_____

_____

What life situation are you currently experiencing where you could demonstrate this kind of love?

_____

_____

_____

_____

_____

 ASSIGNMENT:

• It's been noted that 1 Corinthians 13 paints a composite picture of the person and character of Jesus Christ. Please reread this chapter replacing the word "love" with the word "Jesus." As you do, meditate upon any new insights into the character of Christ which comes to you.

_____

_____

_____

_____

• Think of one person into which you need to pour some of this 1 Corinthians 13 kind of love:

_____

_____

LOVING OTHERS

The Bible's most succinct definition of love can be found in 1 John 4:16, "GOD IS LOVE!" Simple, to the point, complete, easy to remember: God is love! Notice that it doesn't say, "God does love when He feels like it." Not! God *IS* love!

And in the manifestation of who and what He is, God in His Word proclaims love toward a needy world. The golden text of the Bible says, "For God so loved the world that He gave His one and only Son that whoever believes in Him shall not perish but have eternal life" (John 3:16). That's where we have come into the equation. God loved us into His kingdom.

The toughest thing about love is being loving to others. Some people are easy to love, but what about those unlovely people, those enemies? How is it possible to love like God loves? It's an impossibility for us normal human beings. It can't be done alone. It can only be done in the power of the Spirit and the transformation of the human spirit.

A pastor relates the following true story: During vacation Bible school my wife had an experience with her primary class that she says she will never forget. Her class was interrupted on Wednesday about an hour before dismissal when a new student was brought in.

This little boy had one arm missing and since the class was almost over she had no opportunity to learn any of the details about the cause, or his state of adjustment. She was very nervous and afraid that one of the other children would comment on his handicap and embarrass him. There was no opportunity to caution them, so she proceeded as carefully as possible.

As the class time came to a close she began to relax. She asked the class to join her in their usual closing ceremony. "Let's make our churches," she said, clasping her

Just think of the major impact which could be made in a world hungry for love if we really became the people of Jesus Christ and begin to love like Christ.

hands together, fingers interlocked. "Here's the church and here's the steeple, open the doors and there's. . . ." The awful truth of her own actions struck her. The very thing she had feared the children would do, she had done!

As she stood there speechless, the little girl sitting next to the boy reached over her left hand and placed it up to his right hand and said, "Davey, let's make the church together."[1]

Not a whole lot is going to happen for the good in this world until we can team up with God and other people to make life what it ought to be, church what it ought to be, society what it should be, and homes what they should be. Together, in partnership with God, we can reach out and touch all who might be hurting or incomplete. So — how do we really learn how to love others? Let's take another look at the ultimate chapter on loving others — Luke 10:25–37.

How have you been responding to people in your past who have been hurting?

_____

_____

_____

_____

To whom is Jesus telling this story?

_____

_____

_____

What two questions did this so-called "expert" in the law ask of
Jesus?

_____

_____

_____

Do these two questions have a current application in your life?
If so, why?

_____

_____

_____

_____

Jesus condensed all of the law into two actions — name them:

_____

_____

_____

_____

_____

_____

Why do you think Jesus chose to depict the Samaritan as the hero?

_____

_____

_____

_____

_____

_____

In contrast, why did Jesus use a priest and a Levite as a bad example?

_____

_____

_____

_____

_____

Think of the many ways in which this life action was costly to the Samaritan:

_____

_____

_____

_____

_____

_____

Does this story have anything to do with race, ethnics, religions, or nationalities? If so, explain:

_____

_____

_____

_____

Would you be willing to cross any of the above mentioned barriers to help someone in need? If you did, what might it cost you?

_____

_____

_____

How do you handle the "go and do likewise" command?

_____

_____

_____

_____

Be honest — what kind of lifestyle changes should you make so that you can become a good Samaritan to others?

_____

_____

_____

_____

 ASSIGNMENT:

• Think of one person or one family who at this moment are the people on the side of the road in a world of hurt:

_____

• Now — what life action or actions could you take to treat them as a "neighbor"?

_____

_____

_____

_____

SOME OF THE MARKS OF LOVE
AS A FRUIT OF THE SPIRIT

It was an ancient rabbi who asked his students how they could tell when night had ended and day was on its way back.

"Could it be when you see an animal in the distance and can tell whether it is a sheep or a dog?"

"No," answered the rabbi.

"Could it be when you look at a tree in the distance and can tell whether it is a fig tree or a peach tree?"

"No."

"Well, then, when is it?" the students demanded.

"It is when you look on the face of any woman or man and see that she or he is your brother or sister. Because if you cannot do that, then no matter what time it is, it is still night."

So then — what are some of the marks by which love can be measured?

_____

_____

_____

_____

It will enable you to love your enemies! This benchmark is from Matthew 5:43–48. Read it again. In fact, here is a reason for maturity or perfection. This expression is so far beyond the ordinary expressions of natural love that there is no doubt that the Spirit of God is at work in you. It is a very special kind of love manifestation.

Moffat translates verse 47 this way: "If you only salute your friends, what is special about that?" J.B. Phillips translates this verse: "Are you doing anything exceptional?"

The Christian is to manifest, to show, to act on, a very special, exceptional kind of life action — by loving an enemy or enemies! Such a love removes all doubt. The person expressing this kind of love is exhibiting the kind of love Jesus showed. A beautiful illustration of this principle takes place at the martyrdom of Stephen when he says, "Lord, do not hold this sin against them" (Acts 7:60). This is a genuine fruit of the Spirit in action!

Love changes the character of the people who love! You simply cannot express this kind of love without being changed yourself. That is the power of this supreme fruit of the Spirit. It isn't only objective — it is subjective. It is an impossibility to love others and still remain unlovely yourself. There are too many people who have accepted Christ as Savior who still have hearts that are hard and cold toward others. Here is the answer. As the Spirit of God works with the seed which has been planted and the recipient is obedient, love actions soon melt any hardness of heart.

One prime example of how this works is from the life of John the Beloved, also known as the "Apostle of Love." All of his writings are filled with admonishments to love one another. Yet it was not always a character trait of John's. Perhaps you recall that on more than one occasion Jesus had to deal with James and John, who were nicknamed the "sons of thunder." John was more than willing to call fire down from heaven to destroy an entire Samaritan village. This was anything but a loving attitude.

But in later years, after the Spirit of Christ had been breathed into him following the Resurrection, and years of following the teachings of Christ, all of that was changed in him. The thunder may have remained, but it became a passionate love for others, a supreme loyalty to Jesus Christ, and a love for the truth. Yes — when you love and as you express love you will experience a dynamic change in your own lifestyle. This is an action of the Spirit in your obedient life.

You will be able to love the unlovable! There are lots and lots of people in this world who would not be considered an enemy. These may do us no harm, yet these are people whom we have a hard time loving. We might not hate them, we just dislike them. They may be like running fingernails over a chalkboard in your life — irritating.

Who are these people? Quite easy — these are the people you'd rather avoid being around. There are individuals as well as classes of people we just don't like. Maybe they are socially impaired, ill-mannered, loud, slick, not trustworthy, or uncouth.

Without manifestation of this kind of love, would we have missionaries? Would there be hospitals? Would churches have built colonies where lepers are cared for? Would there be hospice ministries? Would there be ministries to AIDS victims? Would there be shelters for abused women and children? Natural philanthropists have done much in these kinds of areas, but shouldn't the Christian go the second mile?

So the crucial test is the capacity to love all kinds of people. It is the fruit of the Spirit at work making real changes in this world.

I have wept in the night
For the shortness of sight
That to somebody's need
   I was blind.
But I never have yet
   Felt a twinge of regret
For being a little too kind.
         (Author is unknown)

You will be able to live an unselfish life! One of the major curses of our day is this obnoxious trend to "me-first-ism." Ours is the "me first" generation. We need to admit it and come clean — we are being drowned in the philosophy of gross selfishness. Go to any bookstore and look at the self-help shelves, tune into any of the TV or radio talk shows, go to any entertainment venue and see how we have immersed ourselves in pleasing #1. Just because you have become a Christian doesn't mean that you are free from selfishness

We don't like to admit it, but most of us as Christians are faced with the challenge to show some of this love to the unlovely. The great commands to love our neighbors are not limited to people we naturally take a liking to.

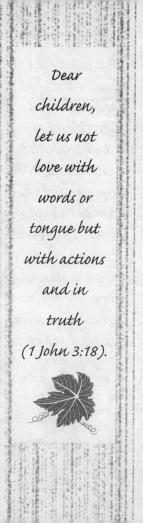

Dear children, let us not love with words or tongue but with actions and in truth (1 John 3:18).

and pride. Lots of Christians are fighting this battle.

Jesus showed us how to really live for others. He gave up all the glories of heaven so that He could be born in the most humble of circumstances to show us the way to living the unselfish life.

Inherently we are born selfish — it is only by the work of the Spirit of God in our internal parts that allows us to live for others.

Here is the test, straight to the point: "This is how we know what love is: Jesus Christ laid down his life for us. And we ought to lay down our lives for our brothers. If anyone has material possessions and sees his brother in need but has not pity on him, how can the love of God be in him? Dear children, let us not love with words or tongue but with actions and in truth" (1 John 3:16–18).

The only way that we can love like this is because of the work of the Spirit working on our own spirit, our own attitudes, our own selfish actions.

This fruit of the Spirit, in the bottom line, is really a harvest for others!

THE PRACTICAL APPLICATION OF THE TRUTH WE HAVE DISCOVERED

Booker T. Washington said: "I will not permit any man to diminish my soul to hatred." In the practical application of truth we come not to discovering how the rubber is to hit the road. In the nitty gritty world where we live, regardless of another's actions, we must be concerned that our reactions always reflect the fruit of the Spirit in the real world.

Ask yourself:

> Am I patient?
> Am I kind?
> Am I generous?
> Am I humble?
> Am I courteous?
> Am I good tempered?

Regardless of what another person's actions may be? Too many of us will likely give a negative answer to such questions. Why?

Let's make our way through another Word study, this time from the practical pen of the Apostle Peter, who learned many a life-lesson on how to live and apply the truth of Spirit-filled living. Read 1 Peter 3:8–18.

To whom is Peter addressing this portion of the Word? (Please don't overlook his use of the phrase "all of you.")

_____

_____

_____

What does "live in harmony with one another" mean to you?

_____

_____

_____

_____

_____

Is it really possible to live in harmony with people who don't agree with you or who might even dislike you? If so, explain:

_____

_____

_____

_____

Does the word "sympathetic" mean anything special to you?

_____

_____

_____

Please explain how it is possible to "love as brothers":

_____

_____

_____

_____

Please define the word "compassionate" as it appears here:

_____

_____

_____

How could you apply compassion to your real world relationships?

_____

_____

_____

_____

Is it more important to "be" compassionate or to "act" compassionate? Explain:

_____

_____

_____

_____

The Bible is the best commentary on the Bible. Therefore, take some time to write out the relationship between repaying or not repaying insults with blessings:

_____

_____

_____

Can you point out some eternal consequences for earthly actions?

_____

_____

_____

_____

Is there a major key in this passage as to how these love actions become a reality for the Christian?

_____

_____

_____

What is your most important life-lesson or truth-application from this passage?

_____

_____

_____

_____

_____

_____

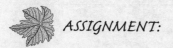 *ASSIGNMENT:*

• How do you plan to put to practical living the truths of this lesson?

_____

_____

_____

_____

_____

• If you are a married person, write down how you plan to implement this kind of living in your home.

_____

_____

_____

_____

• If you are single, write down how you plan to implement this kind of living in your relationships.

_____

_____

_____

_____

A LOVE THAT FORGIVES

Have you ever made a statement similar to this one: "Okay, I will forgive you but I will not forget"? We are now engaged in one

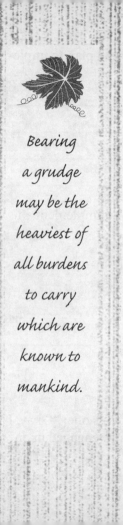

Bearing a grudge may be the heaviest of all burdens to carry which are known to mankind.

of the most exciting aspects of love — FOR-GIVENESS! To forgive or not to forgive, that is the question. But first, a true story to set the tone for this section of study:

On a cold wintry evening a man suffered a heart attack and after being admitted to the emergency room in the hospital asked the nurse to call his daughter. He explained, "You see, I live alone and she is the only family I have."

The nurse went to phone the daughter. The daughter was quite upset and shouted over the phone, "You must not let him die! You see, Dad and I had a terrible argument almost a year ago. I haven't seen him since. All these months I've wanted to go to him for forgiveness. The last thing I said to him was 'I hate you.'" The daughter cried and then said, "I'm coming now — I'll be there in thirty minutes."

The patient went into cardiac arrest and "code blue" was sounded. The nurse prayed, "Oh, God, his daughter is coming. Don't let it end this way." The efforts of the medical team to revive the patient were fruitless. The nurse observed one of the doctors talking to the daughter outside the room. She could see the pathetic hurt on her face.

The nurse took the daughter aside and said, "I'm sorry."

The daughter responded, "I never hated him, you know. I loved him, and now I want to go see him."

The nurse thought, *Why put yourself through more pain?* But she took her to the room where her father lay. The daughter went to the bed and buried her face in the sheets as she said goodbye to her deceased father. The nurse, as she tried not to look at this sad goodbye, noticed a scrap of paper on the bedside table. She picked it up and read: "My dearest Janie, I forgive you. I pray you will also forgive me. I know that you love me. I love you, too. Daddy."[2]

The hurts that have arisen out of holding on to wrongs are incalculable. Bearing a grudge may be the heaviest of all burdens to carry which are known to mankind. So you have really been wronged and it hurts and you may have made the choice to keep your hurt and create a plan of revenge. That kind of life action will only prolong and increase the pain. So how does a person deal with such things?

Where do we go for ultimate answers? Once more back to the words of Jesus Christ — read Matthew 18:21–35.

Have you ever been deeply hurt and
allowed unforgiveness to remain in
your spirit? What happened to your
inner person?

_____

_____

_____

_____

_____

In this parable, why do you think Peter
was so concerned about how many
times forgiveness was to be offered?

_____

_____

_____

_____

_____

Would you like to speculate as to what the reaction of Christ's listeners would have been to such an edict?

_____

_____

_____

_____

Do you think Christ really meant that we should offer forgiveness up to 490 times?

_____

_____

What relationship was Peter referring to when he asked about how many times to forgive? (verse 21).

_____

_____

_____

_____

Let's take time out and do some simple mathematical equations referred to in this parable: Ten thousand talents equals how many dollars? (The clue — a talent in weight was approximately 75 pounds. If these were gold talents, there are 12 "troy" ounces to the pound. So we are dealing with about 9 million ounces of gold — or take the time to figure it out if these were silver talents. The debt is astronomical. Well, you take it from here, figure it out, have fun.)

One more mathematical equation — what is a denarius worth? (The clue — it was approximately a day's wage for a common laborer. In today's system of money, it was worth about 9¢!) And how large was this man's debt?

_____

_____

_____

_____

_____

_____

Why do you think it was so hard for the man who had been forgiven such a large debt to be forgiving to his fellow man?

_____

_____

_____

_____

What are the principles of forgiveness in this parable?

_____

_____

_____

_____

How costly is it to be unforgiving?

_____

_____

_____

_____

Why were the other servants so greatly distressed by the actions taken?

_____

_____

_____

_____

Jesus began this parable by saying, "Therefore, the kingdom of heaven is like. . . ." Make the contrast between the principles of the kingdom of heaven and the kingdom of this world, as pictured here:

_____

_____

_____

_____

_____

_____

_____

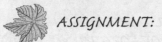 *ASSIGNMENT:*

• Think — is there any relationship you might be involved with presently or out of your past, that needs forgiveness so healing can take place?

_____

• Write out the steps you will take in offering forgiveness:

_____

_____

_____

_____

_____

NOW — just do it! Discipline yourself to put your forgiveness into a life action! Do it before you lose your resolve! Do it before it is too late!

> *The grace to forgive comes from God — the decision to forgive is ours! And what a harvest of this fruit of the Spirit for others as well as for ourselves! Eternity may hinge on it!*

A LIFE APPLICATION OF THIS PRINCIPLE OF FORGIVING LOVE IN ACTION

The late Corrie ten Boom is an example of the truth of forgiveness. She had been stuck for years in a concentration camp during World War II. There she had been humiliated and degraded, especially in the "delousing shower" where the women prisoners were ogled by the leering, lecherous guards. She somehow made it through that living hell and eventually, by the grace of God, she felt she had even forgiven those fiends who guarded the shower stalls.

So she preached forgiveness — for individuals, for nations, for all of Europe. She preached it in the United States. One Sunday in Munich, after her message, greeting people, she saw a man coming toward her, hand outstretched, "Ja, Fraulein, it is wonderful that Jesus forgives us all our sins, just as you say."

THEN!!! She remembered his face — it was the leering, lecherous, mocking, taunting face of an SS guard in the shower stalls.

Her hand froze at her side — she could not forgive! She thought she had forgiven all. But she could not forgive when she met the guard, standing in the flesh in front of her. Ashamed, horrified at herself, she prayed: "LORD, FORGIVE ME, I CANNOT FORGIVE!"

As she prayed, she felt forgiven, accepted, in spite of her shabby performance as a "world-famous-forgiver." Her hand was unfrozen, the ice of hate melted, her hand went out to his. She forgave as she was forgiven! And I suspect, she would not be able to sort out the difference.

Forgiveness is outrageously costly, yet the only way to true peace with God and with others is in an honest act of forgiveness. Our only escape from history's cruel past and unfairness is the miracle of forgiveness. This is the act which opens eternity to us.

A LOVE THAT LASTS FOREVER!

How long should LOVE as a fruit of the Spirit last? Jesus pointed out a problem about living in the "last days." Well, let's just read the verse from Matthew 24:12: "Because of the increase of wickedness, the love of most will grow cold." Do you think that we are living in days of "cold love"? That is a frightening prediction. And at the same time Jesus holds up that the supreme standard of our relationships with each other will be based on our love for each other (John 13:34–35).

For these, as well as many other reasons, we must be concerned about how to make our love last from here on into eternity. Once more we refer to the teachings of Jesus and how to live in such a way as to make this love last and remain a "hot" kind of a love.

The story is told about a native Christian who was making an appeal before a denominational missions board about sending missionaries to his land. The question was asked, "What kind of a missionary should we send to your land?"

Without hesitation, he replied, "Send us missionaries with a hot heart!"

The same cry exists in our society. It may not be articulated, but I believe there is an inherent hunger in people to see and experience real love lived out in a Christian's life.

For our next study on this facet of love, please read John 15:5–17.

To whom is Jesus speaking in this passage?

_____

_____

_____

What is this kind of love as Jesus defines it here?

_____

_____

_____

_____

_____

What are we capable of doing without him?

_____

_____

_____

_____

Discuss the relationship of a vine with its branches:

_____

_____

_____

_____

In verse 9, Jesus professes His love for us. In what ways has this love been modeled in the life of Christ?

_____

_____

_____

_____

What is the greatest kind of expression of love that is possible?

_____

_____

_____

_____

What is the key word in living out a love that lasts? Define that word:

_____

_____

_____

_____

_____

What is the distinction between "friends" and "servants"?

_____

_____

_____

_____

_____

_____

_____

What are the steps of progression a person will be taking when becoming a new Christian to a Christian that bears lasting fruit?

_____

_____

_____

_____

_____

_____

Explain what it means to you that you have been chosen to bear fruit:

_____

_____

_____

_____

_____

_____

Is there a difference between being "chosen" and being "appointed"? If so, please explain what you think is the distinction:

_____

_____

_____

_____

_____

The bottom line in this scripture passage reads: "This is my command: LOVE EACH OTHER!" How can we do this and fulfill His command? (Did you notice that this is a command and not a suggestion?)

_____

_____

_____

_____

_____

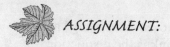

ASSIGNMENT:

• Write out your own personal plan on the action steps you will be taking in order to bear fruit that lasts:

_____

_____

_____

_____

• What do you think will be the results when you as an individual and together with your church really begin to unleash this fruit of the Spirit into all of your relationships?

_____

_____

_____

_____

_____

IN SUMMARY

We have learned or re-learned a number of things about love and perhaps, something about ourselves. It really comes down to the decision we all must make: To love or not to love, that is the question.

God is love and commands His children to live in love, grow in love, mature in love, share in love, and show to the world the difference that love in living can make.

Here is a working definition of love: LOVE is an action directed to another person that is motivated by our relationship to Jesus Christ and is given freely without a personal reward in mind!

And so, in this study, we have been confronted with one of the greatest choices in life: To love or not to love; to love in word or to love in action; to live a

LOVE is an action directed to another person that is motivated by our relationship to Jesus Christ and is given freely without a personal reward in mind!

selfish life or a self-less life; to live for God or to live for self; to live for others or to live for selfish interests.

The greatest rewards in life come out of a lifestyle lived in love. Together, let's make the following commitments:

- The first commitment is to love God with heart, mind, and soul.
- The second is to commit to a life of bearing the fruit of love.
- The third is to learn how to love your neighbor as yourself.

Isn't it amazing that God has chosen us as instruments in order to funnel His love through us for others? We are to become a delivery system for God's love. My prayer is that your life will forever be changed because of this study and the positive steps you have taken that will enable you to live in LOVE!

Let's conclude with another story of love in action, a true story. This happened in the Ravensbruck concentration camp, where during World War II, Nazis put to death some 92,000 women and children. It was a "Good Friday" and a group of women were lined up for the gas chamber. One of them became hysterical. From the crowd of other women, not chosen for death on that day, a figure emerged and approached the woman broken by fear and hysteria. She said, "It's all right. It's all right. I'll take your place."

That woman was Elizabeth Pilenko, who came from a very wealthy family in the south of Russia and eventually became a nun to work among the poor of that region. During the war, the convent in which she ministered became a safe house for many fleeing Jews. When the Gestapo came to the convent, on a tip from an informer, "Mother Maria" (as Elizabeth Pilenko was called) was arrested and sent to Ravensbruck. There she made a lasting impression on other prisoners — even the guards spoke of her as "that wonderful Russian nun."

I don't really understand how one human being can take the place of another condemned to death, other than that this is an action of the fruit of the Spirit working out in human form.

Jesus said: "I am the good shepherd . . . and I lay down my life for the sheep. . . . The reason my Father loves me is that I lay down my life. . . . No one takes it from me, but I lay it down of my own accord" (John 10:14–18).

Jesus also said:

A NEW COMMAND I GIVE YOU: LOVE ONE ANOTHER, AS I HAVE LOVED YOU, SO YOU MUST LOVE ONE ANOTHER. BY THIS ALL MEN WILL KNOW THAT YOU ARE MY DISCIPLES, IF YOU LOVE ONE ANOTHER (John 13:34–35).

And the fruit of the Spirit is . . . LOVE!

1   Jeanie Stoppel, *Parables, Etc.*, February 1984, Saratoga Press.
2   Edwin Evans, *Parables, Etc.*, June 1984, Saratoga Press, p. 2.

Nine Fruits of the Spirit

Study Series includes

Love

Joy

Peace

Patience

Kindness

Goodness

Faithfulness

Gentleness

Self-Control

Robert Strand

Retired from a 40-year ministry career with the Assemblies of God, this "pastor's pastor" is adding to his reputation as a prolific author. The creator of the fabulously successful Moments to Give series (over one million in print), Strand travels extensively, gathering research for his books and mentoring pastors. He and his wife, Donna, live in Springfield, Missouri. They have four children.

Rev. Strand is a graduate of North Central Bible College with a degree in theology.